S*p*ider
Relatives

WRITTEN BY PETER J. PATTERSON

Written by Peter J. Patterson
Photography by Peter J. Patterson and Beren A. Patterson
Additional photography by **Philip Chapman** (scorpion, pages 4-5; scorpion main pic., pages 16-17; long-tailed whip scorpion, short-tailed whip scorpion, and whip scorpion with babies, pages 26-27); **Ray and Lyn Forster** (pseudoscorpion with babies, pages 22-23); **South American Pictures** (spider relative figure, pages 30-31); **Auckland observatory, New Zealand** (constellation of Scorpio, pages 30-31).

© 1995 Shortland Publications Inc.

03 02 01 00 99 98
11 10 9 8 7 6 5 4 3

All rights reserved.

Published by Shortland Publications Inc.
Produced by Shortland Publications,
2B Cawley Street, Ellerslie, Auckland, New Zealand
Distributed in Australia by Rigby Heinemann,
a division of Reed International Books Australia Pty Ltd.
ACN 001 002 357, 22 Salmon Street, Port Melbourne, Victoria 3207
Distributed in the United Kingdom by Kingscourt Publishing Limited,
P.O. Box 1427, Freepost, London W6 9BR

Printed through Bookbuilders Limited, Hong Kong.

ISBN: 0-7901-0992-1

Contents

Cousins, Aunts, and Uncles	4
Amazing Legs	6
Gathering and Shedding	8
Jaws, Armour, and Poison Gas	10
A Confusion of Words	12
Tails of the Night	16
Dangerous Pets	18
Tiny Cousins without a Tail	20
Zoo in a Lunch-box	22
The Greatest Bite on Earth	24
Nervous Hunters	26
The Mighty Mites	28
Stories and Stars	30

Cousins, Aunts, and Uncles

Spiders are not the only creatures with eight legs. They belong to a much larger group of eight-legged animals called the arachnids, or spider relatives. You will never get tired of looking for these interesting creatures. Like me, I think you will find them completely fascinating.

A few arachnids, like the poisonous scorpions, are already famous. In this book, I want to tell you more about the famous ones, as well as introduce you to some of the others.

Harvestmen are the easiest arachnids to find, unless you live in extreme conditions, such as a hot desert or near the North and South Poles.

This is an unusual, short-legged harvestman that lives under a big stone just below my kitchen window. I call him *Jaws*.

AN ELEGANT BUT VERY POISONOUS SCORPION FROM THE MULU CAVES IN SARAWAK (BORNEO)

A LONG-LEGGED HARVESTMAN FROM THE SOUTH OF INDIA

Amazing Legs

Most harvestmen that run around in gardens have small jaws, but unbelievably long legs. Imagine that your arms and legs are only half as thick as they really are. Then imagine that they are ten or eleven times longer. Now try to run! And by the way, your eyes are right up on top of your head, so you cannot see where you are putting your feet. No wonder harvestmen often appear to move in a jerky, clumsy fashion.

The first time I examined a harvestman, I was struck by the tidy pattern its legs make underneath the head, where the legs all grow very close together. That, too, must feel very different from the way our arms and legs grow from either end of our bodies.

One of the strangest things about these delicate legs is the way their owner can drop them to avoid danger. A missing leg will not grow again, but the harvestman does not seem to mind too much, as long as the sensitive second pair of legs is not damaged.

Alert and ready to go – a European harvestman is about to make a run for it.

This harvestman's legs fit into strong, white sockets, which are arranged very close together under its body, four on each side.

Sometimes you can find an old harvestman hobbling around on its remaining legs.

Gathering and Shedding

A harvestman's body does not have a clearly defined waist like a spider's body. A harvestman has no silk glands and, therefore, cannot spin a web. It hunts its dinner, but will also eat decaying animals, the gills of mushrooms, bread and milk, and even jam or marmalade. Most of these are things a spider would find quite disgusting.

A harvestman is not venomous, so when it hunts, it has to kill by sheer force. When it leaps onto its prey, such as an insect, the harvestman will often seize it with all eight legs at the same time, then slam its body down like a hammer to knock out its victim.

Throughout its life, every time it has a growth spurt, a harvestman needs to shed its skin. Spiders are very quiet and patient while they are waiting to do this, but a harvestman will shake itself furiously until its skin splits. Then the really hard part begins. It has to be very careful now, and pull its legs out slowly, one by one, from inside the old skin, which has become stiff and brittle. This can take a long time.

A harvestman has only two eyes, instead of a spider's eight.

This old harvestman ate most enthusiastically when it was offered bread soaked in milk.

Harvestmen usually feed by hunting other animals, such as flies. Most of them are not terribly fussy about what they eat.

Jaws, Armour, and Poison Gas

Once I watched a large spider trying to attack a rather harmless-looking harvestman. To my surprise, the spider backed off, rubbing its eyes with its front legs. It looked as if it was in pain.

Harvestmen can defend themselves by spraying a strong-smelling fluid from the sides of their bodies. This spray acts like a poison gas on many smaller creatures, which quickly learn to leave harvestmen alone.

So far, I have been telling you about the sort of harvestmen you can find in your garden. In damper, darker places, such as caves and ancient forests, they often look quite different. The cave- and forest-dwellers tend to be more angular in shape, and are usually covered in tough plates of hardened skin, like tiny, prehistoric monsters.

Many cave-dwelling harvestmen have rows of fearsome spikes on their *palps* or *palpi*, the short limbs on either side of their mouths. These palps can grow larger and develop into deadly weapons.

A SHORT-LEGGED HARVESTMAN FROM NEW ZEALAND NATIVE BUSH

Some harvestmen have powerful legs, as you can see on this magnificent harvestman from a cave in South America. When I tried to pick it up, it nipped me by snapping its back legs together!

A Confusion of Words

I often hear people talk about harvestmen as daddy-long-legs. This is a good description apart from the fact that half of them are mummy-long-legs! People often refer to the pholcus spiders, which live in houses almost all over the world, as daddy-long-legs. Large crane-flies, those clumsy insects that come indoors on warm evenings, are sometimes given the same name, too. So you can never be sure what people mean when they say daddy-long-legs.

Let's have a look at these three very different creatures. The pholcus is responsible for most of the cobwebs in our houses. Among the arachnids, only spiders spin snares of silk, so the pholcus must be a spider, not a harvestman.

Even without a web, you can see at a glance how to classify the different animals. The long-legged type of harvestman has a round body all in one section, while the pholcus, like all spiders, has a body divided into two clear parts, with a very narrow waist.

MALE PHOLCUS SPIDER SHOWING BODY IN TWO SECTIONS

FEMALE PHOLCUS SPIDER WITH EGGS THAT SHE CARRIES IN HER MOUTH

This harvestman looks a bit like a pholcus spider with part of its body missing. However, the bodies of harvestmen are always only one section.

A Confusion of Words
(continued)

Because they are insects, not arachnids, crane-flies are different again. They have only six legs. Like the pholcus, they also have a narrow waist, but they have a thin neck, too, so you can clearly distinguish the head from the body.

And there are the wings, of course! No arachnid has wings, but there is something peculiar about a crane-fly's wings. Most insects, like dragonflies or butterflies, have four wings, but crane-flies belong to the true flies, or diptera, along with mosquitoes and the common housefly. Look at a crane-fly the next time one comes whirring in, and you will see it has only two big wings. The second pair, as with all diptera, is reduced to tiny stubs.

A crane-fly's eyes are larger and more complicated than arachnid eyes, another difference that you can see at a glance. Try examining this insect's eyes with a good magnifying glass, or through a binocular microscope.

Crane-flies are usually rather dull creatures, but a few of them are quite stunning, like this emerald green one I found in my garden in New Zealand.

Tails of the Night

Among the most impressive of the spider relatives are the scorpions. Some of them are no more poisonous than a bee or wasp, while others are as dangerous as a cobra or rattlesnake.

A scorpion's venom is in the tip of its tail, but it can do more with that tail than just sting. If the scorpion wants to enlarge its home, it will dig out a hole with its front legs. Then, when it has a pile of dirt, the scorpion uses its tail like a broom to sweep everything neatly away.

Although they prefer to live in warm countries, scorpions usually spend the day under a large stone or log to avoid harmful, direct sunlight. Scorpions come out after dark, and appear to make little use of their eyes. Their vision is thought to be very poor.

Scorpions carry their tails curled forward above their bodies, ready for use. The bulb near the end of the tail contains a gland that makes the poison. The point is the sting itself.

Like all scorpions, this fat-tailed scorpion from North Africa has two main eyes, right in the middle of its head. It actually has six more eyes at the front edge of its face. They are tiny and very hard to see.

Dangerous Pets

Most scorpions prefer to kill their prey by biting them. They use the sting in their tail only as a last resort. However, there are exceptions to this rule, and you must be extremely careful if you decide to look after a scorpion.

The most striking thing about scorpions is their huge palps, which are equipped with powerful claws, or pincers. In most cases, scorpions with thin pincers are very poisonous, while those with broad pincers give a sting about as painful as that of a bee or wasp.

To build a home for a scorpion, you will need some dirt or sand and a log for the roof. Scorpions do not eat very often, so they need to be fed only once every 10-15 days. Your pet will sicken and die if you feed it too much. It will, however, need to drink daily. Keep a piece of cotton wool soaked in water from which your pet can suck moisture.

At 20 cm, this African scorpion is one of the biggest in the world.

The narrow claws of the yellow scorpion are a warning that the sting from this creature's tail will cause almost certain death. In contrast, I found this enormous but relatively harmless scorpion, with very fat pincers, in the jungle in Sri Lanka.

Tiny Cousins Without a Tail

Collect a jar of rotting leaves from a damp place under some bushes or trees. Spread the leaves in a thin layer on a large sheet of paper, then stay still and watch. All sorts of creatures, such as centipedes, tiny insects, slaters, and spiders, will come out to see what is happening. Be patient – the most interesting creatures of the forest floor will hold out for the longest time.

We are looking for the little pseudo-scorpions – "pseudo" meaning false. They are just like the big scorpions, except that they have no tail at all. One famous naturalist called them "the most fascinating animals on Earth", so don't miss the pleasure of studying them. They are, however, among the smallest arachnids, usually measuring no more than 3-4 mm.

When you first spread out the leaves, pseudo-scorpions will draw in their limbs. Wait, and you will see them unfold themselves and begin wandering about slowly. They wave their long palps enquiringly, sometimes holding them up like antlers. Try touching their claws very gently, and watch them scurry backwards.

Another unusual habit is that of hitching rides. A pseudo-scorpion will often hang on to a leg of an insect or harvestman and travel for long distances.

Searching through leaf litter for pseudo-scorpions requires a lot of patience. They are tiny and can keep still for quite a long time.

The pseudo-scorpion's poison is made in the bulbs on its claws. It nips little insects with its pincers, injecting them with venom.

Zoo In A Lunch-Box

A flat, plastic lunch-box is ideal for looking after pseudo-scorpions. Put some damp dirt at the bottom, and cover it with rotting leaves and a stone or a piece of bark. Keep the lid on most of the time or the contents will dry out, and your tiny pets will die.

Pseudo-scorpions need to feed once or twice a week, and like their big cousins, they are completely carnivorous. They will eat only tiny, live insects. Put a fresh cupful of rotting leaves in the lunch-box every week and your pets will soon find a meal in this material.

These creatures keep their venom in their long front claws. Judging by its effect on small insects and spiders, a nip from their claws must be very poisonous indeed. They are much too tiny to be able to bite us, though, and can be handled quite safely.

Like spiders, pseudo-scorpions spin silk, but the threads come out of their mouths, or to be more precise, out of the end of their tiny jaws. Under the protective cover of bark or stone, they spin a silk house that is round and white like an igloo. Female pseudo-scorpions make good mothers and feed their babies with a type of milk.

This pseudo-scorpion is running backwards, something at which they are surprisingly good.

A pseudo-scorpion's babies are pure white. The mother feeds them with a nourishing liquid that she makes inside her own body. Her offspring will stay with her inside the silk igloo until they can fend for themselves.

The Greatest Bite on Earth

One of the liveliest animals I know is the solfugid, or sun spider. These energetic creatures can be found racing along at a breathtaking speed in the warm deserts of North America, Africa, and the Middle East. They are as big as a large spider, and for their size, they are among the fastest runners in the world.

Solfugids are excellent fighters, too. Not even tarantula spiders or scorpions stand a chance against them. They are not poisonous, but their bite carries more power for their size than the jaws of an alligator.

Sun spiders are unbelievably enthusiastic eaters. A baby solfugid, only 5 mm long, can eat up to one hundred flies a day! The adults will eat large insects, lizards, mice, and even birds.

Sun spiders have suckers on their palps and can climb up glass. An empty aquarium with some dry sand and rocks to burrow under makes a good home, but do not forget the cotton wool and water. And remember to keep the lid on!

Solfugids are easily identified by their creamy orange legs and head, and their long jaws. Two black eyes stand up above their heads, giving their faces a very eager look.

Nervous Hunters

Whip-scorpions are very large, too, but they are quite the opposite of the sun-loving solfugids. They like to spend the day in dark places, especially in damp caves or forests. Most of them are rather shy.

There are two main groups: those with tails and those without. One of the largest of the tailed whip-scorpions lives in the southern United States where they will often come into people's houses. They can give a nasty nip with their huge, spiky palps. The bite is not poisonous, but if you get too close, they may spray you with an acid gas, which smells like vinegar. (Don't let it get in your eyes!)

The whip-scorpions without tails are the flattest of all arachnids. They also have the longest front legs of any animal I know. Once, when I tried to look at one, it scurried towards a crack in a tree, which I was sure was much too narrow for such a big creature. But it disappeared without effort.

This long-tailed whip-scorpion can spray out an acid in self-defence. The spray's vinegary smell has earned the scorpion the nickname "vinegaroon".

Whip-scorpions are good mothers. Like wolf spiders and true scorpions, they carry their many babies around on their backs until the young are old enough to look after themselves.

The Mighty Mites

Mites and ticks go where other arachnids cannot venture, from the most remote mountain tops to the salty depths of the sea. Most of them are very small, but they include some of the most colourful of the spider relatives.

Scientists spend a lot of time studying these tiny creatures. Some mites are beneficial to nature, and help forests produce a healthy and nourishing topsoil. Many of them, however, are harmful. Gardeners know that the "red spider", a tiny mite that races around on leaves, can kill whole trees. Other mites carry terrible illnesses, such as paralysis, Texas cattle fever, and Kenya typhus.

Not many people are particularly fond of mites, but in fact, they can be fascinating to watch. I always carry a good magnifying glass so that I can see these and the many other little animals that can be found outdoors.

SHEEP TICK

This red mite, which I photographed in Scotland, looks like a tiny harvestman as it walks through a bed of lichens on the forest floor.

Cattle ticks will often stay on an animal's body, sucking blood for several hours. Then they will drop off into the grass to breed.

Stories and Stars

Arachnids have played a fascinating part in the folk-tales and religions of ancient civilizations. In an Egyptian myth, for example, the goddess Isis sets out on a quest, accompanied by an unruly bodyguard of seven giant scorpions.

In the legend of Gilgamesh, which was once the most popular story in the Middle East for a record-breaking 2,000 years, the entrance to the world after death was guarded by "scorpion-men", who were half-human and half-scorpion.

If you look into the night sky, you can find the stars of the scorpion. I think Scorpio is the most majestic of all constellations, but in ancient times, it was even more impressive than it is today, because it included the constellation of Libra, or the Scales. Once, those stars were the "claws of the scorpion" that accompanied Virgo on her journey across the sky.

Both North and South America have many arachnid myths, too. The ancient desert pictures from Peru include a huge, but amazingly accurate, drawing of a ricinuleid. This is a slow-moving, blind spider relative that still lives in that part of the world.

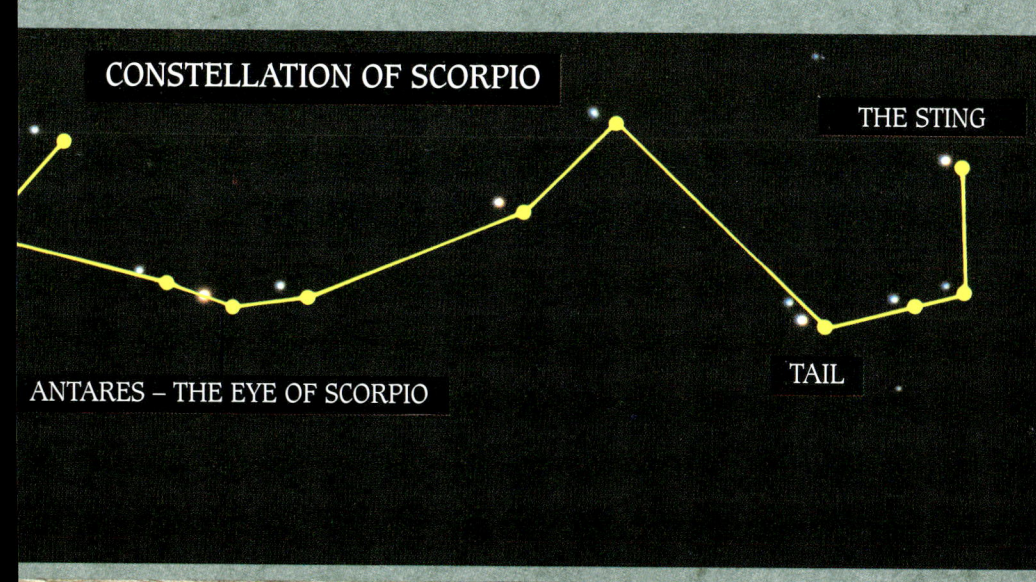

CONSTELLATION OF SCORPIO
THE STING
TAIL
ANTARES – THE EYE OF SCORPIO

SPIDER RELATIVE FIGURE, NAZCA LINES, PERU

TITLES IN THE SERIES

SET 9A

Television Drama
Time for Sale
The Shady Deal
The Loch Ness Monster Mystery
Secrets of the Desert

SET 9B

To JJ From CC
Pandora's Box
The Birthday Disaster
The Song of the Mantis
Helping the Hoiho

SET 9C

Glumly
Rupert and the Griffin
The Tree, the Trunk, and the Tuba
Errol the Peril
Cassidy's Magic

SET 9D

Barney
Get a Grip, Pip!
Casey's Case
Dear Future
Strange Meetings

SET 10A

A Battle of Words
The Rainbow Solution
Fortune's Friend
Eureka
It's a Frog's Life

SET 10B

The Cat Burglar of Pethaven Drive
The Matchbox
In Search of the Great Bears
Many Happy Returns
Spider Relatives

SET 10C

Horrible Hank
Brian's Brilliant Career
Fernitickles
It's All in Your Mind,
    James Robert
Wing High, Gooftah

SET 10D

The Week of the Jellyhoppers
Timothy Whuffenpuffen-
    Whippersnapper
Timedetectors
Ryan's Dog Ringo
The Secret of Kiribu Tapu Lagoon